PIANO_VOCAL_GUITAR

_KINGS_OF_LEON_  >ONLY_BY_THE_NIGHT >

ISBN 978-1-4234-8872-9

HAL•LEONARD®
CORPORATION

7777 W. BLUEMOUND RD. P.O. BOX 13819 MILWAUKEE, WI 53213

In Australia Contact:
Hal Leonard Australia Pty. Ltd.
4 Lentara Court
Cheltenham, Victoria, 3192 Australia
Email: ausadmin@halleonard.com.au

Visit Hal Leonard Online at
www.halleonard.com

CLOSER

Words and Music by CALEB FOLLOWILL, NATHAN FOLLOWILL,
JARED FOLLOWILL and MATTHEW FOLLOWILL

Moderately slow

CRAWL

Words and Music by CALEB FOLLOWILL, NATHAN FOLLOWILL,
JARED FOLLOWILL and MATTHEW FOLLOWILL

You

broke ___ my mouth, ___ the blood - y bits are spit - tin' out. _____ Is your
rat ___ and the fly, ___ they're search - ing for an al - i - bi. _____ As we

D.S. al Coda

SEX ON FIRE

Words and Music by CALEB FOLLOWILL, NATHAN FOLLOWILL,
JARED FOLLOWILL and MATTHEW FOLLOWILL

Con - sumed _____

with what's to tran - spire. _____

USE SOMEBODY

Words and Music by CALEB FOLLOWILL, NATHAN FOLLOWILL,
JARED FOLLOWILL and MATTHEW FOLLOWILL

Syncopated Rock

Oh, _____ oh.

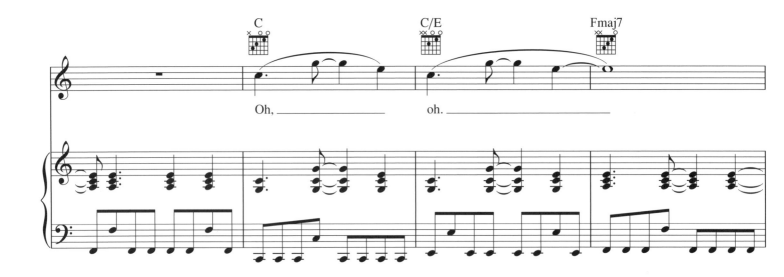

Oh, _____ oh.

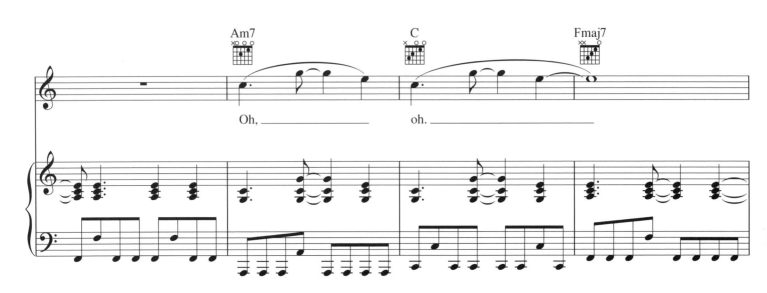

Oh, _____ oh.

MANHATTAN

Words and Music by CALEB FOLLOWILL, NATHAN FOLLOWILL,
JARED FOLLOWILL and MATTHEW FOLLOWILL

Moderately

I like to dance all night, fuel the fire. Gon-na

sum-mons the day. ___ But that's ___ how I play, yeah, that's ___
stoke it up. ___ We're gon-na sip this wine and

keep on   and then for - ev - er ___ roam. ___

REVELRY

Words and Music by CALEB FOLLOWILL, NATHAN FOLLOWILL,
JARED FOLLOWILL and MATTHEW FOLLOWILL

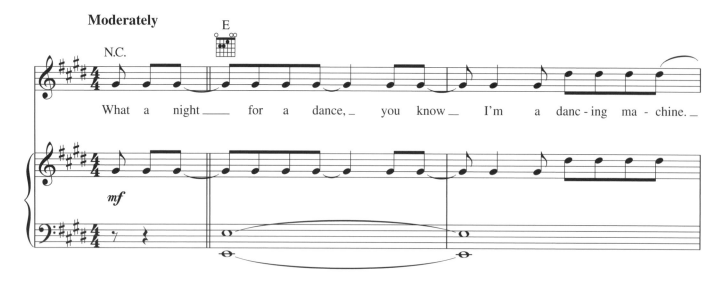

What a night ___ for a dance, ___ you know ___ I'm a danc-ing ma-chine. ___

— With a fire ___ in my bones ___ and the sweet—

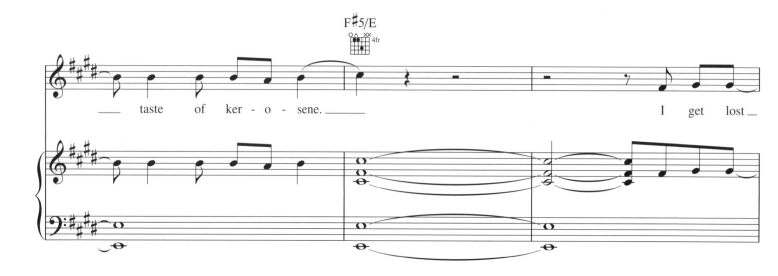

— taste of ker-o-sene. ___ I get lost—

17

Words and Music by CALEB FOLLOWILL, NATHAN FOLLOWILL, JARED FOLLOWILL and MATTHEW FOLLOWILL

Oh, ___ she's on-ly sev-en - teen. ___

NOTION

Words and Music by CALEB FOLLOWILL, NATHAN FOLLOWILL,
JARED FOLLOWILL and MATTHEW FOLLOWILL

I WANT YOU

Words and Music by CALEB FOLLOWILL, NATHAN FOLLOWILL,
JARED FOLLOWILL and MATTHEW FOLLOWILL

Moderately

Fick - le fresh - man, _ prob -'ly thinks she's cool - er than you. _

A hay ride, _ a fire. _ Ev -'ry - bod - y's com - in' a - round. _

So go press _ your skirt. _

Word is there's a new girl in town. _

I call __ shot - gun, __ you can play your R & B tunes. __
Home-boy's __ so proud, __ he fi - n'ly got the vid - e - o proof. __

__ The fel - low - ship time, __ it
__ The night vi - sion shows __

al - ways comes a lit - tle too soon. __ The
she was on - ly duck - in' the truth. __ It's

And, ba - by, this is on - ly bring-in' me down.

BE SOMEBODY

Words and Music by CALEB FOLLOWILL, NATHAN FOLLOWILL,
JARED FOLLOWILL and MATTHEW FOLLOWILL

some - bod - y. _____

Now ___

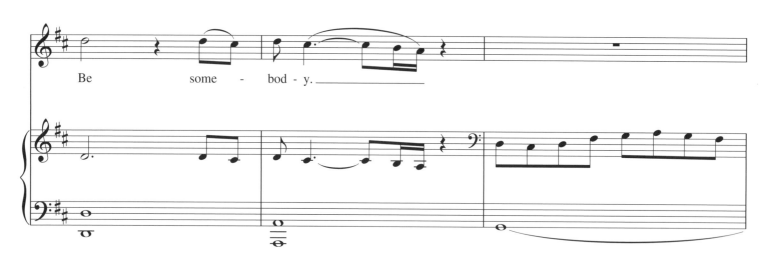

Be some - bod - y._____

Be some - bod - y._____

N.C.

COLD DESERT

Words and Music by CALEB FOLLOWILL, NATHAN FOLLOWILL,
JARED FOLLOWILL and MATTHEW FOLLOWILL

I'm _____ on the cor - ner _____ wait - ing for _ a light _ to come _ on. _____
Told _____ me you loved me, _____ that I'd nev - er die a - lone. _____
I've _____ nev - er ev - er _____ cried when I _____ was feel - in' _____ down. _____

That's when _ I know that _____ you're a - lone. _____
Hand o - ver your heart, _ let's go _____ home. _____
I've al - ways been scared _ of the _____ sound. _

It's cold ___ in the des - ert, ___ wa - ter nev - er sees ___ the ___ ground. ___
Ev - 'ry - one no - ticed, ___ ev - 'ry - one ___ has seen ___ the ___ signs. ___
Je - sus don't love me. ___ No one ev - er car - ried ___ my load. ___

Spe - cial ___ un - spo - ken ___ with - out ___ sound.
I've al - ways been known ___ to cross ___ lines.
I'm too ___ young to feel ___ this ___ old. ___

Ah. ___